INTRO TO PHYSICS Need to Know

SilverTip

Light and Sound

by Jane Parks Gardner

Consultant: Kathy Renfrew
Science Educator and Science Learner

BEARPORT
PUBLISHING

Minneapolis, Minnesota

Credits

Cover and title page, © Dudbrain/iStock and © Photoimpuls/Shutterstock; 4–5, © Gary Miller/Getty Images; 7, © Tooykrub/Shutterstock; 10, © Somchai Som/Shutterstock; 11, © Andrey tiyk/Shutterstock; 13, © Iakov Kalinin/Shutterstock; 14, © Shukaylova Zinaida/Shutterstock; 15, © Pat_Hastings/Shutterstock; 16, © Nataliia K/Shutterstock; 17, © Dzmitrock/Shutterstock; 18–19, © Scott Book/Shutterstock; 20, © Science Photo Library/Alamy; 22, © Jurik Peter/Shutterstock; 23, © Chayanin Wongpracha/Shutterstock; 25T, © Daniel Jedzura/Shutterstock; and 25B, © YoloStock/Shutterstock; and 27, © oatawa/Shutterstock.

Bearport Publishing Company Product Development Team

President: Jen Jenson; Director of Product Development: Spencer Brinker; Senior Editor: Allison Juda; Editor: Charly Haley; Associate Editor: Naomi Reich; Senior Designer: Colin O'Dea; Associate Designer: Elena Klinkner; Product Development Assistant: Anita Stasson

Library of Congress Cataloging-in-Publication Data is available at www.loc.gov or upon request from the publisher.

ISBN: 979-8-88509-222-7 (hardcover)
ISBN: 979-8-88509-229-6 (paperback)
ISBN: 979-8-88509-236-4 (ebook)

Copyright © 2023 Bearport Publishing Company. All rights reserved. No part of this publication may be reproduced in whole or in part, stored in any retrieval system, or transmitted in any form or by any means, electronic, mechanical, photocopying, recording, or otherwise, without written permission from the publisher.

For more information, write to Bearport Publishing, 5357 Penn Avenue South, Minneapolis, MN 55419. Printed in the United States of America.

Contents

Who's Ready to Rock? 4
All about Waves 8
Light It Up 10
What's Next? 12
Cool Colors 16
Hear the Energy 18
Knock, Knock 22
Sound versus Light 24

Light and Sound Waves 28
SilverTips for Success 29
Glossary 30
Read More .31
Learn More Online 31
Index 32
About the Author 32

Who's Ready to Rock?

The lights go off and excitement builds. A drumbeat begins to pulse. Soon, a guitar joins in, followed by a voice singing along. Lights begin to flash in time with the beat. The concert has begun! This is all possible because of **energy**.

Energy lets things do work. It may make something move or change temperature. There is energy almost everywhere, from a home kitchen to a rock concert.

Flashing lights and thumping music may seem like very different things. One you see, and the other you hear. But they actually have a lot in common. Both are forms of energy. And they both travel from place to place in waves.

Not only can you can hear sound waves. You can also feel them. Sound waves move as vibrations, or small shakes. They travel through air and other objects. This includes your body!

Sometimes, you can feel sound when you're near a speaker.

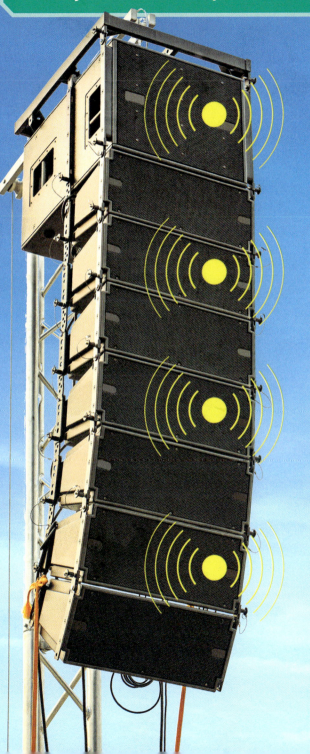

All about Waves

How do waves work? They travel in a repeated pattern as they move the energy. Picture an ocean wave. The highest points above the waterline are its **crests**. The lowest points are the **troughs**. There are many crests and troughs in a wave.

The Parts of a Wave

Wavelength

The height of a wave from its starting point is the **amplitude**. And the distance between two crests or two troughs is called a **wavelength**. These measure a wave's energy in different ways.

Amplitude can be measured from a crest or a trough.

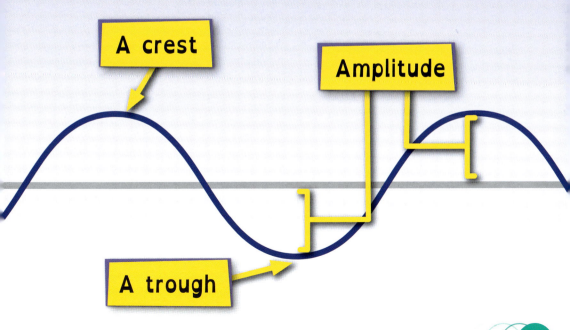

Light It Up

Light often moves a lot like ocean waves. The energy travels up and down in a **transverse wave**. These waves come out of lightbulbs in your home. And light from the sun travels to Earth in these waves. Light waves keep traveling in the same direction until something stops them.

Light is often thought to move in waves. But it also behaves like particles. These little specks of light energy move on their own. Many particles group together to make light.

What's Next?

What happens when light hits something? That all depends on what it hits! Sometimes, light is **absorbed**. It is taken into the object. This happens most frequently with darker colored objects.

> Dark objects often absorb more of the light energy that hits them. This is one reason darkly colored materials heat up in sunlight more than lighter ones. The energy that was light becomes heat.

Dark roadways absorb the sun's light. That's why they are often hot.

Often, when light hits an object, it changes direction. Light from the sun bounces back off our moon. It **reflects** against the moon's surface. This is why our moon seems to glow at night. Light reflects off the surface of objects on our planet, too. It bounces to our eyes to let us see.

Light travels more slowly in water than in air. This makes light waves change direction when they move between air and water. Have you ever seen a straw look like it's bent in a glass of water?

Cool Colors

Light reflecting off objects is how we see colors, too. Light might not look like it has any color. But it is actually a mixture of many colors. Some objects reflect most of the colors in the sunlight that falls on them. Many objects absorb some colors and reflect others. The colors that are reflected are what we see.

A pair of blue sneakers absorbs all the colors in light except blue. Blue is reflected off the shoes. That means we see them as blue.

Hear the Energy

Sound travels in waves, too. The crash of thunder during a storm comes to you in a wave just like the flash of lighting. But you see lighting before you hear thunder. Why? It's because sound waves are different than light waves.

Nothing travels faster than light. On average, light moves at about 186,000 miles per second (300,000 kps). Sound goes only about 0.2 miles per second (0.3 kps).

Unlike light, sound moves in **longitudinal waves**. The waves travel in the same direction as sound's energy. Think of a spring. The vibrating pulse of the wave pushes together and spreads out. This is similar to how coils move in a spring.

Longitudinal Wave

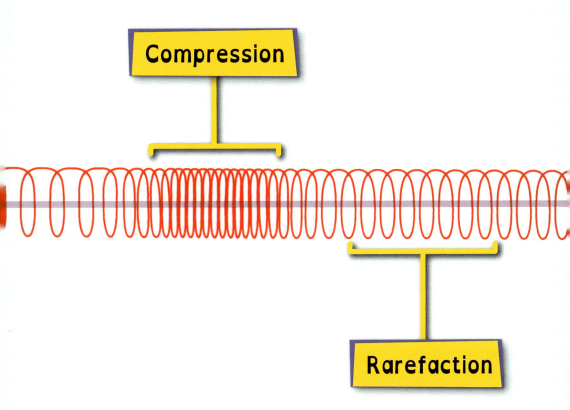

The places in a longitudinal wave that are pressed closest together are areas of compression. These are a lot like a transverse wave's crests. Rarefaction (rair-uh-FAK-shuhn) are places where things are more spread out.

Knock, Knock

Sound waves need to have something to travel through. Sound energy moves through your throat when you speak. Then, the waves go through air. The sound of a knock moves energy through a solid door. Sound travels farther and faster through **denser** objects.

Sound can't travel through space. That's because there's nothing for the sound waves to push together in order to move.

Sound versus Light

Sometimes, we can hear things from places we might not be able to see. Sound travels through a wall. But we can't see light from the other side.

However, unlike light, sound loses energy as it travels. The movement of a sound wave turns some of its energy into heat.

> Sound can travel through objects. But sometimes sound loses energy before it can get to you.

Although they are different, light and sound waves are both forms of energy we need. The sound of an alarm may wake you up. Then, sunlight coming in through the window lets you see as you get ready. Throughout the day, waves of energy help us live our lives.

We have learned to use light as a tool. Lasers focus a lot of light energy into a very small space. They are even strong enough to cut through rocks and metals!

Light and Sound Waves

Sound and light waves both move energy. But they do it in different ways.

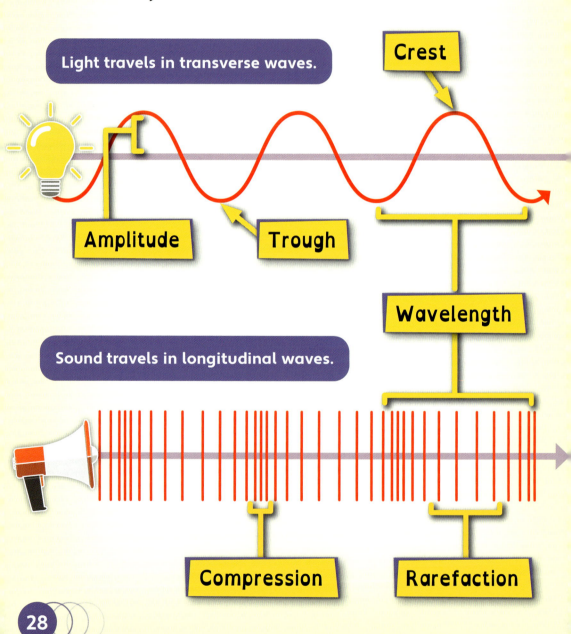

SilverTips for SUCCESS

⭐ SilverTips for REVIEW

Review what you've learned. Use the text to help you.

Define key terms

amplitude
crest
energy
trough
wavelength

Check for understanding

What is similar about sound and light?

How do we see color?

Describe the differences between how longitudinal and transverse waves travel.

Think deeper

How do the different ways sound and light travel change the way you experience these forms of energy?

SilverTips on TEST-TAKING

- **Make a study plan.** Ask your teacher what the test is going to cover. Then, set aside time to study a little bit every day.

- **Read all the questions carefully.** Be sure you know what is being asked.

- **Skip any questions** you don't know how to answer right away. Mark them and come back later if you have time.

Glossary

absorbed taken in or soaked up

amplitude the height of a wave from the midpoint to the top of a crest or from the midpoint to the bottom of a trough

crests the top parts of a wave

denser more tightly packed with things

energy the power to do work, or cause changes

longitudinal waves waves that vibrate in the direction of energy and can move sound

reflects bounces back against something

transverse wave a wave that vibrates up and down to carry its energy and can move light

troughs the lowest parts of a wave

wavelength the distance in a wave between two crests or two troughs

Read More

Haelle, Tara. *Light Waves (Science Masters).* North Mankato, MN: Rourke Educational Media, 2020.

Richards, Jon. *Light and Sound (Science in Infographics).* New York: Gareth Stevens Publishing, 2020.

Stuart, Colin. *The Speed of Starlight.* Somerville, MA: Candlewick Press, 2019.

Learn More Online

1. Go to **www.factsurfer.com** or scan the QR code below.
2. Enter "**Physics Light and Sound**" into the search box.
3. Click on the cover of this book to see a list of websites.

Index

absorb 12–13, 16
amplitude 9, 28
color 12, 16
crest 8–9, 21, 28
light 4, 6, 10–16, 18, 20, 24, 26, 28
longitudinal 20–21, 28
ocean 8, 10
reflect 14, 16
sound 6–7, 18, 20, 22, 24, 26, 28
transverse 10, 21, 28
trough 8–9, 28
wavelength 8–9, 12, 28

About the Author

Jane Parks Gardner has written more than 50 nonfiction books. She spends a lot of her time thinking about, reading about, writing about, and talking about science to anyone who'll listen.